Life is Surprising!

I Talk You Talk Press

CONTENTS

Introduction   1

Story 1: The Earring   2

Story 2: The Dog and the Carpet   8

Story 3: The Visitor   11

Story 4: The Castle   15

Story 5: The Man in the Forest   18

Thank You   23

About the Author   24

INTRODUCTION

This is a collection of short stories for learners of English.

Story 1: The Earring
Story 2: The Dog and the Carpet
Story 3: The Visitor
Story 4: The Castle
Story 5: The Man in the Forest

STORY 1: THE EARRING

Carlos is a taxi driver. He doesn't have much money, so he doesn't own a taxi. Carlos is a driver for a big taxi company. The company owns the taxis. Every day, Carlos drives a different taxi.

Carlos is a very handsome man. Everyone thinks he is very good looking.

Sometimes, women passengers in his taxi say, "What time do you finish work? We are having a party tonight. Would you like to come?"

Carlos gets many invitations for dates from women, but he always says 'no'.

Why does he say 'no'? Carlos says 'no' because he is in love.

He loves Maria. He has never spoken to Maria. He can't speak to her. Her full name is Maria Benedita Gregória. Carlos knows her name because it is on the wall next to her picture. You see, Carlos is in love with a picture of Maria. Maria's picture is in the city art gallery.

Every day Carlos walks to the taxi company. He works from 6:00am to 3:00pm. But Carlos always arrives at work at 5:00am. He arrives early to clean his taxi. The company has a rule. After work, all taxi drivers have to clean the taxi they drove. But many drivers don't clean them. Sometimes the taxi Carlos has to drive is dirty. Carlos doesn't like that. So he cleans the taxi before he starts work.

When Carlos finishes work, he goes to the art gallery. He likes art. But especially, he likes the painting of Maria Benedita Gregória. He stands in front of the painting and looks at it for a long time.

He knows everything about the painting. He bought a catalogue from the art gallery. It has a small photograph of the picture in it. He keeps the catalogue next to his bed. The woman in the picture is very beautiful and young. She is wearing a white satin dress. She has beautiful jewellery - diamonds and emeralds. She is looking out of the picture. Carlos thinks she is looking at him. Carlos dreams that she is still alive. He dreams that she is his girlfriend. It is very sad because Maria Benedita Gregória died in 1929.

Carlos knows it is crazy. He never tells anyone about his secret love. But he knows he will never love another woman. Sometimes, if he is alone in the art gallery, he talks to Maria. He thinks that sometimes she answers him.

One morning, Carlos arrives at work as usual at 5:00am.

"Good morning," he says to the man in the taxi office. "Which car will I drive today?"

"Good morning, Carlos," answers the man in the office. "Number 505 for you today. I'm sorry. Benny drove it last night. It's very dirty. That man is a pig. He never cleans his taxi."

"That's OK," says Carlos. "I have time. I will clean it."

Carlos cleans the outside of the taxi first. Then he starts to clean the inside. Benny was eating in the taxi last night. On the floor next to the driver's seat there are empty cans and an empty pizza box. The back of the taxi is not so dirty, but Carlos cleans that too. Then he sees something shiny. It is on the floor next to the back seat. He picks it up. It is an earring. Carlos looks at it. He thinks, *I know this earring! I have seen this earring before. Maybe I saw a passenger wearing it.*

The taxi company has a rule. If a driver finds anything in the taxi, he has to give it to the man in the office. Then, if a passenger calls and says, "I left my wallet in one of your taxis" or, "I left my coat in the taxi," the man in the office can say, "I have it here," or "I'm sorry, we didn't find it."

But Carlos doesn't want to give the earring to the man in the office. He wants to think about it. He puts the earring in his pocket.

When Carlos finishes work, he takes the taxi back to the company. Then he takes a bus to his apartment. He makes a sandwich and a cup of coffee. He sits down at the table in his small kitchen. He takes the earring from his pocket and looks at it.

Where have I seen this earring? he thinks. He holds the earring in his hand. He thinks for a long time. Then he remembers!

He runs to his bedroom. He takes the catalogue from the art

gallery. He looks at the photograph of the picture of Maria Benedita Gregória. He looks at Maria's earrings.

Yes! That's it! The earring in his hand is the same!

Carlos goes back to the kitchen. He thinks, *This earring has emeralds and diamonds. If they are real jewels, this earring is very valuable. I should give it to the man in the office. But I don't want to. I want to find the owner. I want to give the earring back to the owner myself.*

Carlos eats his sandwich and drinks the coffee. He takes a shower. Then he puts the earring in his pocket and goes downstairs. He takes a bus back to the taxi company. He talks to the man in the office.

"I want to talk to Benny. When will he finish his work today?"

"He will be here at about midnight," answers the man.

Carlos goes to the art gallery. He looks at the painting of Maria Benedita Gregória. He still loves her. He wants to take the earring out of his pocket but he is too scared. Maybe someone will see him. Maybe the earring is made from real diamonds and emeralds. Carlos could be in big trouble.

When the gallery closes, Carlos goes to a park. He sits on a bench in the park. He thinks about the beautiful picture. He thinks about the earring. Then he falls asleep.

When he wakes up it is very late. He looks at his mobile phone. It is 11:40pm. He runs to the taxi company. He waits for Benny. Benny drives his taxi into the garage at five minutes past midnight.

Benny is tired. He wants to go home but Carlos wants to talk to him.

"Benny. Last night. Did you have a woman passenger?"

"Of course. I had many passengers. Some of them were women."

"Tell me about them. Where did you take them?"

Benny is very tired. "I don't know. I can't remember."

"Please Benny! Think!"

"I picked up two women and took them to a restaurant in the Jardins district. I picked up an old man and a woman at the metro station on Rua Vergueiro. They wanted to go to an apartment building near the university. All the other passengers were men. No! I remember. There was one more. I took a young woman to a hotel. She seemed upset. That was my last job last night."

The owner of the earring is the young woman, thinks Carlos. *But why do I think so? This is strange.*

"Which hotel, Benny?"

"I don't remember. Go away. I'm too tired. I want to go home."

Benny walks out of the garage. Carlos thinks, *What should I do?*

Then he remembers. Every time a taxi driver picks up a new passenger, they have to call the office. The taxi company keeps a record of every job on the computer in the office.

Carlos runs to the office. The night-time office manager is a woman called Renata.

"Renata," says Carlos. "Last night, Benny took a woman to a hotel. Which hotel was it?"

"Why do you want to know?" asks Renata.

What should I say? thinks Carlos. He can't tell Renata about the earring.

If he tells Renata, she will say, "Why did you keep it? Give it to me. You know the rule." Carlos might lose his job.

Carlos thinks hard, but he has no idea. Then there is a loud noise in the garage. A taxi coming in has hit a taxi going out. Renata runs out. Carlos can hear her shouting at the drivers.

Quickly Carlos goes to the computer. *I must hurry! Renata will come back soon!*

He finds Benny's last job last night.

---From the Jardim da Luz Park to Hotel Jovem Viajante ---

Carlos goes out of the office. It is too late to go to the hotel now. But tomorrow is Wednesday. Carlos does not work on Wednesdays. He will go to the hotel tomorrow morning.

Early the next morning, Carlos is standing outside the hotel It is a small and cheap hotel. It is for young people with no money.

He thinks, *Only poor people stay in this hotel. So this earring is made of glass and plastic.*

But he wants to see the owner of the earring.

Carlos waits for hours. He watches the people walking into the hotel and out of the hotel. Of course Carlos doesn't know the owner of the earring. He doesn't know her name. He doesn't know her face. But he believes he will find her.

It is 2:00pm. Carlos is tired and hungry.

I have seen many people, he thinks. *But who is the owner of the earring? I still don't know. I am so stupid. What can I do? I will go to the gallery. I will ask Maria Benedita. She will help me!*

Carlos goes to the gallery. When he arrives at the gallery, he feels angry. Someone is standing in front of the picture of Maria Benedita

Gregória. He can't talk to her. He has to wait.

Carlos walks across the room until he is near the picture. A woman is standing in front of the picture. She is young and pretty. She is crying. She doesn't hear Carlos. Then Carlos gets a surprise. The young woman is talking to the picture!

"Oh great-grandmother, I am Barbara. I came here from my home. It is a very small town near Tejupa. I worked in the local shop. I hated it. I want to live in the city but my father wants me to stay at home. I have no mother. My grandmother was very kind. She told my father to let me go to the city. I saved my money. I saved for two years. Finally, I had enough money to come here. Grandmother told me about you. She told me to come and see your picture. She gave me her earrings. She said, 'The earrings will bring you good luck! They are my mother's earrings. Long ago, our family was rich and powerful. But now our family has nothing. We only have the earrings'.

"Last week I got a job in the city. It was an office job. I started looking for an apartment. But I did a terrible thing. A man at the office asked me to go on a date with him. I said 'yes'. I wore the earrings because I wanted to look beautiful. But the man from the office is not a nice man. He didn't take me to a restaurant. He took me to a park. I was scared and I ran away. I got a taxi. When I got to my hotel I looked in the mirror. I was very shocked. I only had one earring. I cannot go back to that office. I cannot go home. I don't know what to do! I am so sorry."

Carlos waits. He is sure the picture will talk to Barbara. He looks at the picture. But the eyes in the picture are not looking at Barbara. The eyes in the picture are looking at him!

What does this mean? Carlos asks himself. *Maria Benedita wants me to do something. But what? What does she want me to do?*

Carlos suddenly shouts, "Maria Benedita. Tell me! What should I do?"

The young woman turns around. "Who are you?" she asks.

"I am Carlos. I drive a taxi. I have something for you."

Carlos puts his hand in his pocket. He takes out the earring and gives it to her.

"Is this yours?" he asks.

She takes the earring and looks at it for a long time.

"Yes! It is! This is a miracle! Where did you find it? How did you find me?"

Carlos says, "I like this painting. When I found the earring, I thought it looked the same as the earring in the painting. I came to check."

Carlos thinks it is not a good idea to say more. If he tells Barbara the whole story, she will think he is crazy. And she is very pretty. She is more beautiful than Maria Benedita.

Then Carlos says, "Would you like to come and have a coffee with me?"

Barbara smiles. "Yes. I would like that. But first I have to do something."

She turns back to the painting. "Thank you great-grandmother. You have helped me. I will come and see you often."

Barbara and Carlos walk towards the door of the gallery. Carlos turns around to look at the painting. Barbara doesn't see him, but he waves his hand to Maria Benedita.

"Goodbye!"

And Carlos is sure that the woman in the painting smiles and waves goodbye back to him.

STORY 2: THE DOG AND THE CARPET

Betty has a new car. Well, it is not a new car, but it is better than her old car. Her neighbour, Mr Warkowsky, died a few weeks ago. The car was Mr Warkowsky's. Before he died, he wrote a letter to his lawyer. He wrote,

---*When I die, give my car to Betty.*---

The car is ten years old, but Mr Warkowsky didn't use it very much. He drove it to church on Sundays, and once a week to the supermarket. So it is almost new. Betty is pleased.

Betty liked the old man. When he got sick, she cleaned his house, did his laundry, and bought food for him. When he died, she was very sad. She went to the funeral. There were very few people there. She was very surprised when the lawyer wrote her a letter.

The letter from the lawyer said,

---*Mr Warkowsky has given all his money to his church, but he wants you to have his car.*---

But there was a problem. Mr Warkowsky also gave Betty his dog.

Benji, the dog, is old and smelly. He lay all day long on a small carpet in Mr Warkowsky's kitchen.

Betty did not want the dog, but she took him. But Betty has a plan. She will keep the dog for a week or two. Then she will take him to an animal shelter. She will say to the lawyer, "The dog has died!" The dog is very old. So the lawyer will not be surprised.

So Benji and his carpet come to Betty's house.

Betty doesn't want the carpet. It is so dirty she can't see any pattern on it. It smells too. But Benji won't be with Betty very long.

When she takes Benji to the animal shelter, she will take the carpet too.

The people at the animal shelter will throw the carpet away, thinks Betty.

But then, a strange thing happens. After a week, Betty starts to like having a dog. When she comes home from work, Benji barks and wags his tail. He stands up and walks to the door to meet her. He lies on the floor in front of her chair in the evenings. They watch television together. She talks to the dog about her day at work, and the dog wags his tail.

Betty decides to keep Benji. But the problem is the dirty carpet.

One Saturday, Betty decides to wash the carpet. She gives Benji an old blanket and he seems to be happy with the blanket. Then she puts the carpet in the washing machine. When she takes it out, there is a lot of dirt at the bottom of the machine.

The carpet looks cleaner, but it is still a little dirty, thinks Betty.

She cleans out the washing machine, and then washes the carpet again. Then she hangs it outside in the garden to dry. She forgets about it.

About 7:00pm, Benji and Betty are watching television as usual. There is a knock at the door. It is the man who bought Mr Warkowsky's house. He is holding Benji's carpet in his hand.

"Hello," says the man. "I'm Adam Findleton. I have just moved into the house next door."

"I know," says Betty. "I'm Betty Wilkins. Can I help you with something?"

"No," says the man, smiling. "But, it's this carpet. You left it outside on the clothesline. You should not do that."

"Why not?" asks Betty. "It's very old and it was dirty. I washed it."

Adam looks very surprised.

"But don't you know what it is? I am an antiques salesman, and I know a lot about carpets. This is a Mohtashem carpet from Iran. It's very old and very precious."

"Is it expensive?" asks Betty.

Adam laughs. "It's a very small carpet, but I think it is worth about fifteen thousand dollars!"

"What?" shouts Betty. "The dog has been lying on it! I didn't know it was so expensive!"

"If you want to sell it, I can sell it for you," says Adam.

"Just a minute," says Betty.

She goes into the house and talks to Benji. She tells Benji about the carpet. Benji wags his tail and barks once.

Betty goes back to the door, Adam Findleton is waiting.

"Yes!" says Betty. "Sell the carpet! Benji and I are going to take a long vacation!"

STORY 3: THE VISITOR

Min-ji is in hospital. Yesterday, when she was going to university, she fell off her bicycle. It was raining. Her bicycle slipped on wet grass. She hit her head on the ground.

Now, she is lying in a hospital bed. She cannot move, and she cannot speak. The nurse gave her lots of medicine. Min-ji feels very sleepy. Her mother and father are with her. They are talking with the doctor.

"When can she come home?" asks Min-ji's mother.

The doctor looks at Min-ji's file. He looks at the X-ray of her head.

"I don't know," he says. "She hit her head on the ground really hard. There is some damage. We have to do some more tests."

"Will she be OK?" asks Min-ji's father.

The doctor looks at Min-ji's father. "I cannot answer that question. We need to do some more tests."

The doctor leaves the room. Min-ji's mother starts to cry. Min-ji looks at her mother, but she cannot speak.

"We'll visit you tomorrow," says her father. "Try and get some rest."

Min-ji tries to say 'goodbye', but she cannot.

They hug Min-ji and leave the room.

Min-ji looks around the hospital room. It is very quiet. She is alone. The late afternoon sun comes through the window. The sun is warm and bright. Min-ji wants to close the curtains, but she cannot. She closes her eyes and falls asleep.

Min-ji wakes up. The curtains are closed. It is very dark in the room. She looks at the clock. It is 3:00am.

She hears something move in the room.

What is that? she thinks. Then she sees a light.

It is a nurse. The nurse has a candle. She is looking at Min-ji's file.

That's strange, thinks Min-ji. *Why does she have a candle?*

The nurse looks at Min-ji. She smiles.

Min-ji smiles at the nurse. Then, she looks at her uniform. The nurse's uniform is different from the other nurses. It looks old-fashioned. The skirt is very long.

"How are you feeling?" asks the nurse.

"My head hurts," says Min-ji.

The nurse looks at the file. Then, she writes something on a piece of paper.

"You will be fine," she says. She walks to the side of the bed. She opens the bedside drawer. She puts the piece of paper inside the drawer.

"What's that?" says Min-ji.

The nurse doesn't say anything. She just smiles. Then, she walks out of the room and closes the door.

Min-ji falls asleep.

The next morning, Min-ji wakes up. There is a nurse in the room. She is opening the curtains.

"Good morning," says the nurse.

Min-ji sits up. "Good morning. Are you the nurse with the candle?"

The nurse looks at her. She is very surprised. Min-ji seems very well.

"Pardon?" says the nurse.

"Last night. There was a nurse in my room. She had a candle," says Min-ji.

The nurse says, "No, there were no other nurses here last night. I was alone. And I don't have a candle."

"But the nurse here at 3:00am had a candle!" says Min-ji.

The nurse smiles. "Min-ji, you have taken lots of medicine. The medicine makes you sleepy. And it makes you dream a lot. You saw the nurse with the candle in a dream."

"I'm going to the toilet," says Min-ji. She stands up and starts walking to the door.

"No! No!" shouts the nurse. "You can't walk!"

But Min-ji is walking fine.

The nurse is very shocked. She shouts, "Doctor! Doctor!"

The doctor comes into the room. He looks at Min-ji.

"Lie down! Lie down!" he shouts.

Min-ji lies down. The doctor looks at her eyes. He looks at the machine next to her bed.

"This is strange," he says to the nurse. "Get a wheelchair."

The nurse brings a wheelchair. They put Min-ji in the wheelchair and take her to the X-ray room.

All the doctors in the hospital look at the X-ray photographs. They cannot believe it.

Min-ji's head is better.

"What happened? What happened?" say the doctors.

"Maybe the nurse with the candle gave me some medicine," says Min-ji.

"Which nurse?" asks the doctor.

"I don't know her name. She came to my room last night," says Min-ji.

The nurse shakes her head.

"No doctor. I was the only nurse here last night. I didn't go into Min-ji's room," she says.

They take Min-ji back to the room.

Later in the afternoon, the doctor says to Min-ji, "You can go home. I will call your mother and father."

Min-ji gets dressed. She puts her items in her bag. She checks the room. *Do I have everything?* she thinks.

She opens the drawer of the bedside table. Inside the drawer, she sees a piece of paper. She looks at it. There is a message on the paper.

---*Min-ji, be careful when you ride your bicycle in the rain. From Kim Chun-ja.*---

Min-ji puts the message in her bag. At the reception desk, Min-ji, and her mother and father say goodbye to the doctors and nurses.

"I have a question," says Min-ji. "Who is Kim Chun-ja?"

"Kim Chun-ja? She was the first nurse at this hospital," says the doctor.

"Does she still work here?" asks Min-ji.

"No, of course not," says the doctor. "She died twenty years ago. But she was a very good nurse. Everyone said, "We feel better when we see Kim Chun-ja.""

"I see," says Min-ji.

"Why do you want to know about her?" asks the nurse.

"No reason," says Min-ji. She smiles and walks out of the hospital into the warm afternoon sun.

STORY 4: THE CASTLE

Celine and Dieter are tourists. They are in Ireland. It is 4:30pm and it is raining.

"What shall we do?" asks Celine.

"Look! There is a castle. Let's go into that castle. I think it's still open," says Dieter.

They walk into the castle.

"Hello," says Shaun, the tour guide. "Would you like a tour around the castle?"

"Yes please," say Celine and Dieter.

Shaun is wearing the clothes of a soldier from hundreds of years ago.

"I like your costume," says Celine.

"Thank you," says Shaun.

"Do all the workers here wear old costumes?" asks Dieter.

"Yes, we do," says Shaun. "But this castle is small, so there are only two workers. The other worker is Patrick."

Shaun takes Celine and Dieter into the main room of the castle. It is very dark and it is very cold. The floor and walls are made of stone. There only a small, narrow window. Celine looks through the window. The rain is very heavy.

"May I take photographs?" asks Dieter.

"Yes, of course," says Shaun. "But it is very dark. You won't get good photographs today."

Dieter takes many photographs. Then, Shaun takes them down some steps into a room under the castle. It is very dark, but there is a small lamp. Shaun switches it on.

"How did people use this room?" asks Dieter.

"They killed people here," says Shaun. "They brought enemies here and killed them. But there is an interesting story.

"One day, a soldier brought a man here. The man was an enemy. But he was very strong. He took the sword from the soldier and killed him. Then, he put the soldier's clothes on and went up the stairs. The other soldiers thought he was the soldier. They didn't know he was the enemy."

"What happened after that?" asks Celine.

"One of the soldiers came down to this room and saw the dead soldier. Then, he understood. He shouted to the other soldiers, 'Kill that man! He is not a soldier! He is the enemy!' But it was too late. The soldiers looked for him, but the man was not here."

"He escaped?" asks Dieter.

"Yes, he escaped," says Shaun.

Dieter takes some more photographs. Then, Shaun takes them back upstairs.

Celine and Dieter say goodbye to Shaun and go back to their car.

Later that night, at the hotel, they look at their photographs on their computer. The photographs are very dark. But one photograph is light and clear.

"Look! Who is that?" asks Celine. She points to a man in a photograph of the room under the castle.

"Is it Shaun?" asks Dieter.

"No, Shaun is here. He is standing next to me."

They look at the photograph more closely. Shaun is standing on the left of the photograph. On the right, there is a man wearing a soldier's costume.

"It's the other guide. It's Patrick," says Dieter.

"I don't remember seeing Patrick," says Celine.

"No, I don't remember seeing him either. But we were listening to Shaun's story very carefully. So maybe we didn't see him," says Dieter. "Shaun said, 'you won't get any good photographs'. But we did get a good photograph. Let's send it to Shaun. He will be very surprised."

Dieter finds the email address for the castle and attaches the photograph. He writes a message to Shaun.

---*Dear Shaun, thank you so much for taking us on a tour today. We had a great time. I took a photograph. It is very light, and we can see you and Patrick on it. We enjoyed your story very much, so we didn't see Patrick in the room! ---*

The next morning, Shaun checks his email. He sees the mail from Dieter. He opens the photograph and looks at it for a long time. Then, he writes an email.

---Dear Dieter and Celine, thank you for visiting the castle yesterday. The photograph is very interesting. Patrick and I enjoyed your visit.---

He doesn't tell Dieter and Celine that he was alone yesterday. He doesn't tell them that Patrick is on vacation in Spain. He doesn't tell them that there was no one else in the room under the castle yesterday. At least no one alive!

STORY 5: THE MAN IN THE FOREST

Christina is a single mother. She works at a bank. She has a son. He is eight years old. His name is David. During the school year, David goes to an after-school club at the community centre. It is very good. Some of his school friends go to the same club. They do their homework together, play games and watch television. When Christina finishes work for the day, she goes to the community centre and collects David. They go home together.

But the school holidays are a problem. Christina has to work, but there is no one to look after David. The after-school club is closed during the holidays.

Christina finds a holiday camp. David can stay at the camp for the long summer holiday. The children at the holiday camp play many sports. They enjoy outdoor adventure activities. David likes fishing and sport, so he is happy at the camp. Christina misses David. The house is very quiet and empty without him.

It is Friday evening and Christina is finishing work. She is walking out of the bank when the telephone rings. It is the manager of the holiday camp.

"I am very sorry," says the manager. "David had an accident. He fell out of a tree. He broke his leg and he hit his head. His leg will be OK, but the hospital is worried about his head. They are doing tests. Please come to the hospital."

Christina runs to the car park and jumps into her car. She is very worried.

I must get to the hospital! she thinks.

The hospital is about 50km away.

If I drive on the new road, it will take me almost 40 minutes. But if I take the old road through the forest, I can get there quicker, she thinks.

A long time ago, people lived in the forest. But no one lives there now. On Saturdays and Sundays, a lot of people use the forest road. Families have picnics in the forest, fishermen go to catch fish in the river, and people enjoy riding their bikes there. But during the week, the forest is empty.

Christina turns off the main road and onto the forest road. She is driving very fast.

I must be careful. I must slow down. I could have an accident, she thinks.

But she is very worried about her son. She can't slow down.

Suddenly the car stops.

"What!" shouts Christina. "What's wrong? Oh no! I don't believe it!"

She looks at the control panel of the car.

"Gas! I've run out of gas! Oh no! I forgot to get gas!"

She looks out of the car window. What can she do? It is dark. She is in the middle of the forest. It is about 10km back to the main road, and about 12km to the other end of the forest.

Should I walk? she thinks. *But if I walk, it will take more than an hour. I have to get to the hospital quickly. Maybe I should call a taxi? Yes! The taxi driver can bring me some gas!*

She takes out her cell phone.

Oh no! There is no signal! I don't believe it! she thinks. *I have to walk.*

She gets out of the car and looks around. *Which way should I walk?*

Just then, she sees a man. He walks between the trees on the side of the road and stands in front of her. He is dressed in work clothes and has an old towel around his neck and the lower part of his face.

He doesn't say anything. He just looks at her.

"Please, can you help me?" says Christina. "My son is in hospital. He had an accident. He fell out of a tree. I have run out of gas! But I must get to the hospital! My son might die!"

The man puts up his hand. He turns and walks back between the trees. Christina watches him. It is dark, but she can see a small house between the trees.

She waits. After about five minutes, the man comes back. He is carrying a very old gas can. Christina jumps into the car and pulls the lever to open the cover to the gas tank. The man pours the gas from the can into the tank.

Christina gets out of the car with her wallet.

"I will pay you for the gas."

She tries to give him a $20 bill. The man steps back and waves his hands at her. He doesn't say anything, but he seems to be telling her 'No!'

The man walks back to the little house. Christina watches him.

Then, she remembers. *David! The hospital!*

She jumps back in the car and drives on through the forest.

It is the next morning. Christina is sitting in a small park next to the hospital with a cup of coffee. David is fine. The hospital did many tests. David's head injury is not serious. He has a broken leg and a headache, but he can leave the hospital on Sunday.

Christina thinks about the man in the forest. He was very kind. She feels bad because he did not take any money for the gas.

I should go back and say 'thank you', she thinks. *I will give him a small present and try to give him some money too.*

Christina goes back into the hospital. David is sleeping. She puts a note next to his bed. The note says:

---*I am going shopping. I will come back soon!*---

Christina wants to buy the man a nice scarf. The man had an old towel around his neck and face.

He needs a scarf, thinks Christina.

Christina goes to a menswear shop and chooses a nice checked scarf. Then she goes to a stationery shop and buys a 'thank you' card. She writes a message in the card and puts $20 into the envelope with the card.

Christina drives to the forest. It is bright and sunny, and there are many bikers and fishermen in the forest.

She stops her car. *This is it,* she thinks. *This is the place where I saw the man last night.*

She gets out of her car and walks through the trees. She looks for the little house. There is no house.

Perhaps this is not the right place, she thinks. *But I'm sure it is near here.*

She walks about 50m. Then, she sees an old man sitting on the grass under a tree. He is eating his lunch.

"I'm sorry to trouble you," she says to the man. "But do you know this part of the forest well? I am looking for a small house. I thought it was very near here."

"I lived here when I was a small boy," says the man. "I've been coming back to fish here for the past forty years. A long time ago, there were houses at the end of the road. But there was only one house here. A man called Bill Aitkens lived in the house."

"Where is Mr Aitkens' house?" asks Christina.

"Bill Aitkens died. Then, the house was empty. It fell down about twenty years ago."

"Where was it?" asks Christina.

"It was right there." The man points to a space. "That area where there are no trees. The house was there."

"What happened to Mr Aitkens?"

"It was a terrible accident. He was a forester, like my own father. One day, he climbed a tree to cut off some of the small branches. He fell. His axe was on the ground and he fell on the axe. His throat was cut."

Christina says 'thank you' to the man and walks away.

Who helped me last night? she thinks. *Not Mr Aitkens. He's been dead for a long time. Maybe I imagined the house. It was dark. Maybe someone was camping near here. Maybe I saw a camping tent.*

She looks at the envelope with the card and money inside and the bag with the scarf. *What should I do?* she thinks. Then, she has an idea. *I will leave the card and the scarf near the place of Mr Aitkens' old house. Perhaps the man will come back.*

She puts the envelope and the scarf in the middle of the area near the place of the old house. Then she drives back to the hospital.

David leaves hospital the next day. When they are driving home, Christina tells David about the gas and the man in the forest.

"Let's go to the forest! Did the man find your present?" says David. "I want to see!"

"Oh, I don't think so," says Christina. "You should be home in bed."

"Oh please! It won't take a long time. You said, 'the forest road is quicker than the new road'. I will be home in bed sooner!"

Christina laughs. "OK. I guess we can drive home that way. But you can't get out of the car."

In the forest, Christina stops the car.

"It was here," she says. "I put the present and the card over there. I'll go and look."

David waits in the car. Soon Christina comes back.

"Were the present and the card still there?" asks David.

"No," answers Christina slowly. "But these were there."

She shows David an old towel and a $20 note.

THANK YOU

Thank you for reading Life is Surprising! We hope you enjoyed the stories. (Word count: 6,203)

If you would like to read more graded readers, please visit our website
http://www.italkyoutalk.com

Other Level 1 graded readers include
A Business Trip to New York
A Homestay in Auckland
A Trip to London
Dear Ellen
Haruna's Story Part 1
Haruna's Story Part 2
Haruna's Story Part 3
Ken's Story Part 1
Ken's Story Part 2
Strange Stories
The Christmas Present
The Old Hospital
We Met Online

ABOUT THE AUTHOR

I Talk You Talk Press is a Japan-based publisher of language textbooks, graded readers and language learning/teaching resources.

Our team is made up of highly experienced language teachers and translators, who have all studied at least one additional language to an advanced level.

This experience enables us to design our materials from the perspective of both the teacher and the learner. We consult with both teachers and language learners when designing our textbooks and graded readers, and test our materials extensively in the classroom before publication.

We are a fast-growing press, and currently publish graded readers for learners of English. We publish new graded readers monthly.